Presented To:

_____

From:

_____

Date:

_____

My First

# 40 Days

with the

# Lord

DESTINY IMAGE BOOKS
PRODUCED IN ASSOCIATION WITH
MAJESTIC GLORY MINISTRIES

*Awakening the One New Man*

My First

# 40 Days

with the

# Lord

MAJESTIC GLORY MINISTRIES

DESTINY IMAGE® PUBLISHERS, INC.
P.O. Box 310, Shippensburg, PA 17257-0310

*"Promoting Inspired Lives."*

This book and all other Destiny Image, Revival Press, MercyPlace, Fresh Bread, Destiny Image Fiction, and Treasure House books are available at Christian bookstores and distributors worldwide.

For a U.S. bookstore nearest you, call **1-800-722-6774.**

For more information on foreign distributors, call **717-532-3040.**

Reach us on the Internet: **www.destinyimage.com.**

ISBN 13 TP: 978-0-7684-4130-7

ISBN 13 Ebook: 978-0-7684-8831-9

For Worldwide Distribution, Printed in the U.S.A.

1 2 3 4 5 6 7 8 / 16 15 14 13 12

# Contact Information

_____

Congregation

_____

_____

Address

_____

Phone

_____

Email

_____

Website

_____

Pastor's name

_____

Hours open

# Contents

Today I accepted Jesus Christ
as my Lord and Saviour

_____

Date

Today I was baptized.

_____

Date

# Welcome

Welcome to the Kingdom of God. Your decision to accept Jesus Christ as your Lord and Savior changes everything. You have been born again. You have now been separated from your sin. Your very name has been written into the Lamb's Book of Life. You have entered into an everlasting life as a child of the living God. This is cause for great celebration in Heaven and on earth.

Jesus came to earth as God's way of demonstrating that He longs to be close to His creation. There is nothing more satisfying than getting to know the love of God. Each day brings the promise of fresh fulfillment with His joy. He is the way, the truth, and the life.

The reason for your first birth has been fulfilled—you have come to know God. Just as a newborn baby has special needs, so does a newborn believer in our Lord Jesus. This is your opportunity to start your new life by learning how to daily walk with our Messiah.

We invite you to make *My First 40 Days With the Lord* a personal record of your honeymoon with the Lord. This will begin a lifelong journey of discovering the depth of your Father's love for all people.

The Word of God has been given to us as a blueprint for living. Within the Bible's pages you will find unending treasures. May this book be your companion as you grow in faith and study the Holy Scriptures.

Many new believers start their Bible reading with the Book of John. Within, you will be able to acquaint yourself with some of the best-known verses from John's Gospel and see how they are intertwined with each of the books of the Old Testament. Our desire is for you to gain both an appreciation for the roots of our faith and revelations of God's design.

We encourage you to carve out a few minutes each day when you can sit quietly and enjoy the presence of our Lord. You will swiftly discover that He awaits you, always.

Godspeed!

# Day 1

## In the Beginning

### JOHN 1:1-5

*In the beginning was the Word, and the Word was with God, and the Word was God. He was with God in the beginning. Through Him all things were made; without Him nothing was made that has been made. In Him was life, and that life was the light of all man. The light shines in the darkness, but the darkness has not understood it* (John 1:1-5).

No one knows more about beginnings than the Creator of the universe. Beginnings determine our purpose and our goals. The Book of John tells us that, *"In the beginning,"* the spoken Word of God became a living being. This living Word was present from the very beginning and was responsible for making everything that was ever made. This life is represented by light. And this light shines in the darkness.

## Reflection

1.  How powerful is the Word of God?

2.  Who was in the beginning with God?

3.  How could everything be made through Him?

### GENESIS 1:1-5

*In the beginning God created the heavens and the earth. Now the earth was formless and empty, darkness was over the surface of the deep, and the Spirit of God was hovering over the waters. And God said, "Let there be light," and there was light. God saw that the light was good, and He separated the light from the darkness. God called the light "day," and the darkness He called "night." And there was evening, and there was morning—the first day* (Genesis 1:1-5).

God created the universe out of a void. There was no form; there were no materials to start with. This was the beginning of all creation. With only a Word, God created light. Next we discover that God said, "It is good."

Then He differentiated between light and darkness. And time began.

## Reflection

1.  How did God create the universe?

2.  Where was the Spirit of God?

3.  Why is there both light and darkness?

# Day 2

# The Coming of the Lord

## JOHN 1:14-18

*The Word became flesh and made His dwelling among us. We have seen His glory, the glory of the One and Only, who came from the Father, full of grace and truth. John testifies concerning Him. He cries out, saying, "This was He of whom I said, 'He who comes after me has surpassed me because He was before me.'" From the fullness of His grace we have all received one blessing after another. For the law was given through Moses; grace and truth came through Jesus Christ. No one has ever seen God, but God the One and Only, who is at the Father's side, has made Him known (John 1:14-18).*

John the Baptist knew Jesus was coming. He knew that a new covenant was being instituted. God's plan was being fulfilled in the flesh. God's covenant given to Moses was displayed on tablets as the Law (see Exod. 32; 34). The New Covenant in Jesus brings us grace, something we could never earn. It has also brought us truth as God displays the promise of His Son in flesh. The eternal God became a human being, just like you and me. Glory!

## Reflection

1. How is it that Jesus came to earth?

2. What do you think grace is?

3. How could John the Baptist know that God's Son was coming?

### DANIEL 9:24-25

*Seventy "sevens" are decreed for your people and your holy city to finish transgression, to put an end to sin, to atone for wickedness, to bring in everlasting righteousness, to seal up vision and prophecy and to anoint the most holy. Know and understand this: From the issuing of the decree to restore and rebuild Jerusalem until the Anointed One, the ruler, comes, there will be seven "sevens," and sixty-two "sevens." It will be rebuilt with streets and a trench, but in times of trouble* (Daniel 9:24-25).

The coming Messiah (Anointed One) was predicted by the works He would perform, as well as the time He would come. By looking for clear signs, prophesied events, and predetermined timing, even a novice could have anticipated the appearance of the Messiah. And thus He came—right on schedule, at the appointed hour, in the fullness of time.

## Reflection

1. Does prophecy, a divine prediction of a future event, really work?

2.  Why would God make a promise about a future event?

3.  What place will be restored before the Messiah comes?

# Day 3

## The Voice in the Wilderness

### JOHN 1:19-23

*Now this was John's testimony when the Jews of Jerusalem sent priests and Levites to ask him who he was. He did not fail to confess, but confessed freely, "I am not the Christ."*

*They asked him, "Then who are you? Are you Elijah?"*

*He said, "I am not."*

*"Are you the Prophet?"*

*He answered, "No."*

*Finally they said, "Who are you? Give us an answer to take back to those who sent us. What do you say about yourself?"*

*John replied in the words of Isaiah the prophet, "I am the voice of one calling in* the desert, 'Make straight the way for the Lord'" (John 1:19-23).

This passage about the voice in the wilderness refers to John the Baptist, who by all appearances was fulfilling the Old Testament prophecy about Elijah. John was preaching the repentance of sin. By repenting of our sin, we prepare ourselves to have an encounter with Jesus, the Messiah of Israel.

## Reflection

1. What is a prophet?

2. How can you tell that John the Baptist is not claiming to be Elijah or a prophet?

3. Who is crying in the wilderness?

## MALACHI 3:1

*"See, I will send My messenger, who will prepare the way before Me. Then suddenly the Lord you are seeking will come to His temple; the messenger of the*

covenant, whom you desire, will come,"
*says the Lord Almighty* (Malachi 3:1).

The children of Israel had been looking for the
Messiah ever since they left Egypt. The language here points to the immediacy of the Lord's soon-coming return. Israel was expectantly listening for the voice. This same voice has called to you. It beckons you to follow.

## Reflection

1.  Can you find, in both passages, the one who is to come?

2.  Does John the Baptist prepare the way for the coming of Messiah?

# Day 4

## The Lamb of God

### JOHN 1:29-34

*The next day John saw Jesus coming toward him and said, "Look, the Lamb of God, who takes away the sin of the world! This is the one I meant when I said, 'A man who comes after me has surpassed me because He was before me.' I myself did not know Him, but the reason I came baptizing with water was that He might be revealed to Israel."*

*Then John gave this testimony: "I saw the Spirit come down from heaven as a dove and remain on Him. I would not have known Him, except that the one who sent me to baptize with water told me, 'The man on whom you see the Spirit come down and remain is He who will baptize with the Holy Spirit.' I have seen and I testify that this is the Son of God"* (John 1:29-34).

The Holy and Righteous God of Heaven and earth wants us to live lives without sin. But humankind has sinned since the beginning of our walk on earth. God, who wants to be close to His creation, needed to give us a way to eliminate this sin so that He can draw near to us. The Lord taught Israel that the forgiveness of sin required a sacrifice. Such a sacrifice must, of itself, be without sin. Only the Son of God could accomplish this.

## Reflection

1. Can the "Lamb of God" be a person?

2. Why would God make a person for sacrifice?

### EXODUS 12:3-8

*Tell the whole community of Israel that on the tenth day of this month each man is to take a lamb for his family, one for each household. If any household is too small for a whole lamb, they must share one with their nearest neighbor, having taken into account the number of people there are. You are to determine the amount of lamb needed in accordance with what each person will eat. The animals you choose must be year-old males without defect, and you may take them from the sheep or the goats. Take care of them until the fourteenth day of the month, when all the people of the community of Israel must slaughter them at twilight. Then they are to take some of the blood and put it on the sides and tops of the door-frames of the houses where they eat the lambs. That same night they are to eat the meat roasted over the fire, along with bitter herbs, and bread made without yeast* (Exodus 12:3-8).

Imagine living under Pharaoh's command. You would be a firsthand witness to ten devastating plagues, and then you would be told to follow these instructions. God went into great detail in guiding His children. He wanted Israel to remember His plan of salvation down through the ages.

## Reflection

1. Why was the lamb without blemish?

2. Why did this lamb stay inside the house from the 10th to the 14th day?

3. What does the blood of the lamb symbolize?

# Day 5

## Follow the Lord

*The next day Jesus decided to leave for Galilee. Finding Philip, He said to him, "Follow Me."*

*Philip, like Andrew and Peter, was from the town of Bethsaida. Philip found Nathanael and told him, "We have found the one Moses wrote about in the Law, and about whom the prophets also wrote— Jesus of Nazareth, the son of Joseph."*

*"Nazareth! Can anything good come from there?" Nathanael asked.*

*"Come and see," said Philip* (John 1:43-46).

The behavior of these men tells us that the Messiah had been expected. Somehow, with only a handful of words, Jesus recruited His disciples. Jesus called His followers to Himself. He simply asked each one to follow Him. Philip identified Jesus as the one Moses and the Prophets wrote about, and he told his friends.

## Reflection

1. Why was Nathaniel skeptical? How did Philip respond to Nathaniel's doubt?

2. Do we know the ways in which God is going to appear to us?

3. Can our expectations about the Lord hamper us?

### 2 CHRONICLES 34:31

*The king stood by his pillar and renewed the covenant in the presence of the Lord—to follow the Lord and keep His commands, regulations and decrees with all his heart and all his soul, and to obey the words of the covenant written in this book* (2 Chronicles 34:31).

Imagine standing in the courtyard of a palace and hearing the king of a nation make a covenant before the Lord to honor Him and His ways. The very idea thrills the soul. A person of authority chooses to honor the highest authority.

## Reflection

1. When was the last time you heard a king or a leader make a covenant to follow the Lord and to keep His commandments?

2. What must we believe to follow a person or to follow God?

3. What happens to a nation that chooses to honor God?

# Day 6

# Three Days

## JOHN 2:18-22

*Then the Jews demanded of Him, "What miraculous sign can you show us to prove Your authority to do all this?"*

*Jesus answered them, "Destroy this temple, and I will raise it again in three days."*

*The Jews replied, "It has taken forty-six years to build this temple, and you are going to raise it in three days?" But the temple He had spoken of was His body. After He was raised from the dead, His disciples recalled what He had said. Then they believed the Scripture and the words that Jesus had spoken (John 2:18-22).*

Jesus knew what was going to happen to Him after His death! He knew that He would be resurrected in three days. He knew His statement about the temple would cause controversy and confusion. He also knew that after His death and resurrection these same words would cause His disciples to remember His bold prophesy.

## Reflection

1. Do you think Jesus wanted to cause confusion about the temple?

2. Why would Jesus want people to remember both the Scriptures and His words?

3. Is it fair for God to challenge our views and beliefs?

### JONAH 1:1-4,15,17

*The word of the Lord came to Jonah son of Amittai: "Go to the great city of Nineveh and preach against it, because its wickedness has come up before Me."*

*But Jonah ran away from the Lord and headed for Tarshish. He went down to Joppa, where he found a ship bound for that port. After paying the fare, he went aboard and sailed for Tarshish to flee from the Lord.*

*Then the Lord sent a great wind on the sea, and such a violent storm arose that the ship threatened to break up... Then they took Jonah and threw him overboard, and the raging sea grew calm... But the Lord provided a great fish to swallow Jonah, and Jonah was inside the fish three days and three nights* (Jonah 1:1-4,15,17).

Jonah was called to go to Nineveh, the Capital of Assyria and the home of the most ruthless, cruel, and tortuous peoples alive. Small wonder that he was hesitant to be God's representative to offer repentance to these sinners. His efforts to avoid this assignment were futile. God gave him three days in the belly of a fish to think about his plight.

# Reflection

1. Do you think Jonah considered himself dead?

2. Why would Jesus compare Himself to Jonah?

3. Can you believe a story like this to be true?

# Day 7

## A New Covenant

### JOHN 3:1-6

*Now there was a man of the Pharisees named Nicodemus, a member of the Jewish ruling council. He came to Jesus at night and said, "Rabbi, we know You are a teacher who has come from God. For no one could perform the miraculous signs You are doing if God were not with him."*

*In reply Jesus declared, "I tell you the truth, no one can see the kingdom of God unless he is born again."*

*"How can a man be born when he is old?" Nicodemus asked. "Surely he cannot enter a second time into his mother's womb to be born!"*

*Jesus answered, "I tell you the truth, no one can enter the kingdom of God unless he is born of water and the Spirit. Flesh gives birth to flesh, but the Spirit gives birth to spirit* (John 3:1-6).

When a Jewish leader named Nicodemus covertly came to Jesus to ask important questions, the answers he received are mindboggling, startling. Jesus told him about things that people have never even considered. Nicodemus struggled to comprehend the magnitude of these declarations.

## *Reflection*

1. Why are signs (miracles) so important?

2. What do they reveal about God?

3. What is different about being born of the Spirit?

### JEREMIAH 31:31-34

*"The time is coming," declares the Lord, "when I will make a new covenant with the house of Israel and with the house of*

*Judah. It will not be like the covenant I made with their forefathers when I took them by the hand to lead them out of Egypt, because they broke My covenant, though I was a husband to them" declares the Lord. "This is the covenant I will make with the house of Israel after that time," declares the Lord. "I will put My law in their minds and write it on their hearts. I will be their God, and they will be My people. No longer will a man teach his neighbor, or a man his brother, saying, 'Know the Lord,' because they will all know Me, from the least of them to the greatest," declares the Lord. "For I will forgive their wickedness and will remember their sins no more" (Jeremiah 31:31-34).*

God promises us that a time will come when He will give His creation a new covenant. This covenant will even surpass the one given at Mount Sinai (see Exod. 24:12). This promise will restore the (now broken) relationship that was given to Israel in the original covenant (see Exod. 20:1-17). We have such a merciful God who forgives us.

# Reflection

1. Why would God make a new covenant with His Creation?

2. What is the difference between the covenant God gave His children in Egypt and this new covenant God promises us via Jeremiah?

3. Why does God tell Jeremiah He will not remember people's sins?

# Day 8

## Salvation

### JOHN 3:13-21

*No one has ever gone into heaven except the one who came from heaven—the Son of Man. Just as Moses lifted up the snake in the desert, so the Son of Man must be lifted up, that everyone who believes in Him may have eternal life.*

*For God so loved the world that He gave His one and only Son, that whoever believes in Him shall not perish but have eternal life. For God did not send His Son into the world to condemn the world, but to save the world through Him. Whoever believes in Him is not condemned, but whoever does not believe stands condemned already because he has not believed in the name*

of God's one and only Son. This is the
verdict: Light has come into the world,
but men loved darkness instead of light
because their deeds were evil. Everyone
who does evil hates the light, and will
not come into the light for fear that his
deeds will be exposed. But whoever lives
by the truth comes into the light, so that
it may be seen plainly that what he has
done has been done through God (John
3:13-21).

Our world has many ideas about love. The
Bible demonstrates love as a sacrificial gift.
Real love costs us everything. God promises us
eternal life based upon our willingness to lay
down our lives for the sake of God's love. God
holds us accountable for being exposed to the
light of His salvation. Our response has eternal
consequences.

## Reflection

1.   Where is Jesus from? How can that be?

2.   What is Jesus' relationship with God?

3. What does God promise those who believe in His Son?

## JOEL 2:28-32

*And afterward, I will pour out My Spirit on all people. Your sons and daughters will prophesy, your old men will dream dreams, your young men will see visions. Even on My servants, both men and women, I will pour out My Spirit in those days. I will show wonders in the heavens and on the earth, blood and fire and billows of smoke. The sun will be turned to darkness and the moon to blood before the coming of the great and dreadful day of the Lord. And everyone who calls on the name of the Lord will be saved; for on Mount Zion and in Jerusalem there will be deliverance, as the Lord has said, among the survivors whom the Lord calls* (Joel 2:28-32).

Joel tells us about God's desires for His children. Times will be tough, but we are instructed to call on the name of the Lord. How remarkable that such a simple act can do so much to change our lives for eternity. Suddenly God does not seem to be so far away. It is quite the opposite; He is close to us, ready to save us. Hallelujah!

## *Reflection*

1. What is so special about the name of the Lord?

2. How can God save someone who calls on His name?

3. Do you believe the world will face such deep turmoil?

# Day 9

## Thirsting for God

### JOHN 4:13-14

*Jesus answered, "Everyone who drinks this water will be thirsty again, but whoever drinks the water I give him will never thirst. Indeed, the water I give him will become in him a spring of water welling up to eternal life"* (John 4:13-14).

Note how the Bible uses such simple illustrations to make such profound statements about our lives and our relationships with God. Everyone knows what it means to be thirsty. Imagine not only having your thirst quenched, but receiving a fountain of water that leads to everlasting life!

# Reflection

1. What type of water is John talking about?

2. How can drinking quench our thirst forever?

3. What is meant by everlasting life?

## OBADIAH 15-16

*The day of the Lord is near for all nations. As you have done, it will be done to you; your deeds will return upon your own head. Just as you drank on My holy hill, so all the nations will drink continually; they will drink and drink and be as if they had never been* (Obadiah 15-16).

In stark contrast to believers who drink from the fountain of eternal life will be those who disregard the holiness of God and His sacred people. Those nations who attempt to conquer will see their schemes turned back against them. These will only drink water that leads to oblivion.

# Reflection

1.  What does the day of the Lord refer to? Why is it near?

2.  Why does God speak of a holy hill? Could this be Mount Zion in Jerusalem?

3.  What happens to people who do not honor God's design?

# Day 10

# Signs and Wonders

## JOHN 4:46-50

Once more He visited Cana in Galilee, where He had turned the water into wine. And there was a certain royal official whose son lay sick at Capernaum. When this man heard that Jesus had arrived in Galilee from Judea, he went to Him and begged Him to come and heal his son, who was close to death.

"Unless you people see miraculous signs and wonders," Jesus told him, "you will never believe."

The royal official said, "Sir, come down before my child dies."

Jesus replied, "You may go. Your son will live."

*The man took Jesus at His word and departed (John 4:46-50).*

Asign or a wonder is a miracle. God knows that we need to see a representation of His wonder-working power. Jesus knew that He was called to demonstrate Heaven's power here on earth. And He did so willingly. Thank you, Lord!

## Reflection

1. How does God build our faith?

2. What does God know about our character?

3. How do you feel when your faith is tested?

## 2 KINGS 6:5-7

*As one of them was cutting down a tree, the iron axhead fell into the water. "Oh, my lord," he cried out, "it was borrowed!"*

*The man of God asked, "Where did it fall?" When he showed him the place, Elisha cut a stick and threw it there, and*

*made the iron float. "Lift it out," he said.
Then the man reached out his hand and
took it* (2 Kings 6:5-7).

Here we see a prophet of God called into
action. An impossible situation was
resolved by a simple act of faith. Imagine the stir
this miracle must have created. Think about the
miracles in your life.

## Reflection

1. How do you react when you see something miraculous?

2. How can an axe head float?

3. Why was the man of God called upon for help?

# Day 11

## The Father's Love

### JOHN 5:19-23

*Jesus gave them this answer: "I tell you the truth, the Son can do nothing by Himself; He can do only what He sees His Father doing, because whatever the Father does the Son also does. For the Father loves the Son and shows Him all He does. Yes, to your amazement He will show Him even greater things than these. For just as the Father raises the dead and gives them life, even so the Son gives life to whom He is pleased to give it. Moreover, the Father judges no one, but has entrusted all judgment to the Son, that all may honor the Son just as they honor the Father. He who does not honor the Son does not honor the Father, who sent Him* (John 5:19-23).

When a father has a genuine love for his off-spring, his generosity is boundless. When a child knows the love of a father, there is true freedom to act without shame or embarrassment. When God becomes your Father, the possibilities are endless—even to the point of raising the dead.

## *Reflection*

1. How deep is a father's love for his children?

2. Did Jesus honor His Father? Did His Father honor Him?

3. Are you willing to do the same?

## SONG OF SOLOMON 7:10-12

*I belong to my lover, and his desire is for me. Come, my lover, let us go to the countryside, let us spend the night in the villages. Let us go early to the vineyards to see if the vines have budded, if their blossoms have opened, and if the pomegranates are in bloom—there I will give you my love* (Song of Solomon 7:10-12).

How wonderful and simple—when we belong to each other, our natural inclination is to think of the one who loves us. We want to bless that person and do marvelous deeds to demonstrate our desire to be with that person. This has been our Lord's intention from the beginning—that we would love one another. True love is often spoken of in terms of possession or belonging. What greater joy is there than to be close to the one we love more than any other—God?

## Reflection

1.  What do you think of walking alongside Father God?

2.  Are you comfortable belonging to Him?

3.  Do you receive His outpouring of love?

# Day 12

## God Reveals Himself

### JOHN 5:37-40

*And the Father who sent Me has Himself testified concerning Me. You have never heard His voice nor seen His form, nor does His word dwell in you, for you do not believe the one He sent. You diligently study the Scriptures because you think that by them you possess eternal life. These are the Scriptures that testify about Me, yet you refuse to come to Me to have life* (John 5:37-40).

We read the Bible because we want to know how God reveals Himself to us in our lives. Often we don't know where or how to find Him. Wise men have long sought to find God and the Messiah within the pages of the Holy

Scriptures. How ironic that, after our long quest, we discover He has always been with us.

## Reflection

1. Have you ever lost or looked for something of great value?

2. Has God revealed Himself to you in His Word?

3. When you study the Holy Scriptures, do you see Jesus?

### NUMBERS 24:15-19

*Then he uttered his oracle: "The oracle of Balaam son of Beor, the oracle of one whose eye sees clearly, the oracle of one who hears the words of God, who has knowledge from the Most High, who sees a vision from the Almighty, who falls prostrate, and whose eyes are opened: I see him, but not now; I behold him, but not near. A star will come out of Jacob;*

*a scepter will rise out of Israel. He will crush the foreheads of Moab, the skulls of all the sons of Sheth. Edom will be conquered; Seir, his enemy, will be conquered, but Israel will grow strong, A ruler will come out of Jacob and destroy the survivors of the city"* (Numbers 24:15-19).

Sometimes the Bible uses language that is unfamiliar to us. Jacob is one of the Bible's names for Israel. Many of the territories surrounding Israel gave them trouble. Moab had a history of strife with Israel. Interesting, the nations occupying the same lands as Moab did often disagree with Israel in these days. In those days, as in our own time, God reveals Himself to save Israel.

## Reflection

1. What is the meaning of *"A star will come out of Jacob"* (see verse 17)?

2. Why does God protect Israel?

3. Is bloodline important to God?

# Day 13

# What Do You Have to Offer?

## JOHN 6:9-11

*"Here is a boy with five small barley loaves and two small fish, but how far will they go among so many?"*

*Jesus said, "Have the people sit down." There was plenty of grass in that place, and the men sat down, about five thousand of them. Jesus then took the loaves, gave thanks, and distributed to those who were seated as much as they wanted. He did the same with the fish (John 6:9-11).*

A young lad made an offering to God. He had enough to feed himself and a few friends, but he offered it all to Jesus. Jesus did more with this small offering than anyone ever could have imagined. Look what God can do with the generosity of just one.

## *Reflection*

1. How do you feel when you are asked to give an offering?

2. What do you think the Lord wants to do with your offering?

3. What does this story tell you about how God blesses His children?

## JOSHUA 5:10-12

*On the evening of the fourteenth day of the month, while camped at Gilgal on the plains of Jericho, the Israelites celebrated the Passover. The day after the Passover, that very day, they ate some of the produce of the land: unleavened bread and roasted grain. The manna stopped the day after they ate this food from the land; there was no longer any manna for the*

*Israelites, but that year they ate of the produce of Canaan* (Joshua 5:10-12).

God miraculously fed the children of Israel manna for 40 years as they walked through the wilderness. Finally, they crossed the River Jordan, entered the Promised Land, and ate of its produce. Israel then celebrated the Passover. The next day, God stopped providing manna, the bread that fell from Heaven, which had sustained Israel in the wilderness for 40 years.

## Reflection

1. Why did God use food to demonstrate His love for Israel?

2. How do you think Israel felt when they entered the Promised Land?

3. How do you feel when God blesses you? Or when God is silent?

4. How important is it that Israel celebrates the Passover?

# Day 14

## Bread and Blood

### JOHN 6:48-54

"I am the bread of life. Your forefathers ate the manna in the desert, yet they died. But here is the bread that comes down from heaven, which a man may eat and not die. I am the living bread that came down from heaven. If anyone eats of this bread, he will live forever. This bread is My flesh, which I will give for the life of the world."

Then the Jews began to argue sharply among themselves, "How can this man give us His flesh to eat?"

Jesus said to them, "I tell you the truth, unless you eat the flesh of the Son of Man and drink His blood, you have no life in you. Whoever eats My flesh and *drinks My blood has eternal life, and I will raise him up at the last day"* (John 6:48-54).

Jesus makes some radical declarations. He likens Himself to heavenly bread and says that Heaven is His home. He tells His followers that they must eat this bread that is His flesh. Then He goes farther, saying that if we don't drink His blood, then we are as good as dead. Then He caps it off by promising eternal life to anyone who will eat His flesh and drink His blood!

## Reflection

1. Who is the bread of life?

2. What does it mean to be living bread?

3. Does Jesus literally want us to eat His flesh and drink His blood?

4. How can eating flesh and drinking blood give us eternal life?

## LEVITICUS 17:11

......................................

*For the life of a creature is in the blood, and I have given it to you to make atonement for yourselves on the altar; it is the blood that makes atonement for one's life* (Leviticus 17:11).

God reveals a portion of His supernatural design. Life is in the blood! When blood is shed, life is poured out. When sacrificial blood is poured upon an altar, the Lord counts this as atonement. This is God's way of allowing us to make amends for our mistakes and failures.

## *Reflection*

1.  Is this really possible? Can a sacrifice cover our sins?

2.  Why would Jewish people object to Jesus asking them to eat His flesh or drink His blood?

3.  Can you understand the dilemma that faces Jewish people when believers in Jesus take communion?

# Day 15

# Righteousness

## JOHN 7:15-19

*The Jews were amazed and asked, "How did this man get such learning without having studied?"*

*Jesus answered, "My teaching is not My own. It comes from Him who sent Me. If anyone chooses to do God's will, he will find out whether My teaching comes from God or whether I speak on My own. He who speaks on his own does so to gain honor for himself, but he who works for the honor of the one who sent him is a man of truth; there is nothing false about him. Has not Moses given you the law? Yet not one of you keeps the law. Why are you trying to kill Me?" (John 7:15-19)*

Jesus was the living Word. He understood the Bible better than the scholars. This was very difficult for the Judean leaders to accept. When He taught them about God, they rejected His teaching. When He taught them about the law that God gave Moses, it troubled them. Jesus said that He was righteous (there is nothing false about Him). His words and actions confounded the scholars of Israel.

## Reflection

1. Is it difficult for you to learn new things about God?

2. How do you think you would have responded to Jesus?

3. How do you tell a person something they don't want to hear?

### AMOS 5:21-24

*I hate, I despise your religious feasts; I cannot stand your assemblies. Even though you bring Me burnt offerings and grain offerings, I will not accept them. Though you bring choice fellowship offerings, I will have no regard for them. Away with the noise of your songs! I will not listen to the music of your harps. But let justice roll on like a river, righteousness like a never-failing stream* (Amos 5:21-24).

Sometimes God tells us that He is not happy with our behavior. He does this because we are missing fundamental truths that He is endeavoring to reveal to His children. This passage does not mean that the Lord doesn't want us to assemble and celebrate His Name. It means that God wants us to live righteous lives. He is more concerned with our walk of integrity than our outward worship of Him. Without humility, there is no honor before God.

## Reflection

1.  What are you learning about righteousness?

2.   Is righteousness the same thing as "right versus wrong"?

3.   What do you need to change to be righteous before God?

# Day 16

## Listen to the Prophet

### JOHN 7:37-38

*On the last and greatest day of the Feast, Jesus stood and said in a loud voice, "If anyone is thirsty, let him come to Me and drink. Whoever believes in Me, as the Scripture has said, streams of living water will flow from within him"* (John 7:37-38).

Jesus cries out to humanity. He calls us to come to Him. He beckons us to drink, to partake of His Spirit. He tells us that our belief in Him will confirm the Holy Scriptures and transform our lives. Out of our own hearts, the very core of our beings, will flow rivers of living water. What an amazing picture of the Holy Spirit at work within us.

## *Reflection*

1. Why does Jesus use the analogy of drinking and the flow of living water?

2. What promise does Jesus make to those who believe in Him?

3. How does this image affect your life as a believer in our Lord Jesus?

### DEUTERONOMY 18:18-19

*I will raise up for them a prophet like you from among their brothers; I will put My words in his mouth, and he will tell them everything I command him. If anyone does not listen to My words that the prophet speaks in My name, I Myself will call him to account* (Deuteronomy 18:18-19).

This is perhaps the most profound forward-looking statement about the coming Messiah that is made in the Torah (the first five books of the Bible).

Consider God using Moses as His chosen prophet—and pointing to a future Messiah, about whom God alone could testify. We not only learn about Him, but we see this prophet, and as His followers, we are required to be obedient to God.

## *Reflection*

1. What does this prophecy given to Moses tell you about God's desire to make and fulfill His promises?

2. How do we know that this prophet is Jesus of Nazareth?

3. When Jesus speaks, does He sound like God?

# Day 17

## The Truth Shall Set You Free

### JOHN 8:31-32

*To the Jews who had believed Him, Jesus said, "If you hold to My teaching, you are really My disciples. Then you will know the truth, and the truth will set you free"* (John 8:31-32).

Father God desires that we would discern and employ His wisdom, as found in the Holy Scriptures. It is these words and Jesus, the Word of God that became flesh, that the Lord refers to when He says, *"If you hold to My teaching...."* The Lord informs us that our yearning to live according to His Word allows us to discern genuine truth and live in freedom. Hallelujah!

# Reflection

1. Did you know that the prerequisite for knowing the truth is living in obedience to God's Word?

2. What does this knowledge do to your understanding of truth?

3. Who alone can set the standard for truth?

## 1 KINGS 3:7-12

*"Now, O Lord my God, You have made Your servant king in place of my father David. But I am only a little child and do not know how to carry out my duties. Your servant is here among the people You have chosen, a great people, too numerous to count or number. So give Your servant a discerning heart to govern Your people and to distinguish between right and wrong. For who is able to govern this great people of Yours?"*

*The Lord was pleased that Solomon had asked for this. So God said to him, "Since you have asked for this and not for long life or wealth for yourself, nor have asked for the death of your enemies but for discernment in administering justice, I will do what you have asked. I will give you a wise and discerning heart, so that there will never have been anyone like you, nor will there ever be"* (1 Kings 3:7-12).

King Solomon humbly asked the Lord to give him the ability to discern between good and evil. Solomon asked to know the truth, for who can discern between good and evil without knowing truth? This request for wisdom so pleased the Lord that God granted Solomon great riches as well.

## Reflection

1. If God asked you what gift you want, what would be your answer?

2. How does God honor people who put Him above everything else?

3. Is your greatest request to be rich or to know the truth?

# Day 18

## Living by Faith

### JOHN 8:53-58

Are You greater than our father Abraham? He died, and so did the prophets. Who do You think You are?"

Jesus replied, "If I glorify Myself, My glory means nothing. My Father, whom you claim as your God, is the one who glorifies Me. Though you do not know Him, I know Him. If I said I did not, I would be a liar like you, but I do know Him and keep His word. Your father Abraham rejoiced at the thought of seeing My day; he saw it and was glad."

"You are not yet fifty years old," the Jews said to Him, "and You have seen Abraham!"

*"I tell you the truth,"* Jesus answered, *"before Abraham was born, I am"* (John 8:53-58).

Abraham is often referred to as "Father Abraham." In the Old Testament, God used Abraham to lay the foundation of faith for the best way to honor God. Jesus told His followers that Abraham rejoiced at the news of the coming Messiah. In this statement, Jesus declared that He had existed even before Abraham. This is such an amazing picture of Abraham's faith fulfilled.

## *Reflection*

1. How could Jesus exist before Abraham?

2. How old is Jesus?

3. How do you think the Judeans responded to such a declaration?

## HABAKKUK 2:4

*See, he is puffed up; his desires are not upright—but the righteous will live by his faith* (Habakkuk 2:4).

Habakkuk speaks of the importance of faith. Note that pride is contrasted with faith. The growth of our faith is the most accurate measure of our spiritual journey through life. As we grow in faith, we grow in our ability to understand and appreciate our relationship with God. The closer we grow to God, the greater our maturity as believers becomes. Mature believers know that pride interferes with our relationship with God.

## *Reflection*

1.  In what way does pride differ from faith?

2.  How does Habakkuk advise us to demonstrate our faith?

3.  How does one "live by faith"?

# Day 19

## I Am the Light of the World

### JOHN 9:1-5

*As He went along, He saw a man blind from birth. His disciples asked Him, "Rabbi, who sinned, this man or his parents, that he was born blind?"*

*"Neither this man nor his parents sinned," said Jesus, "but this happened so that the work of God might be displayed in his life. As long as it is day, we must do the work of Him who sent Me. Night is coming, when no one can work. While I am in the world, I am the light of the world"* (John 9:1-5).

Hebrew tradition held that sickness or affliction was the result of a person's sin. Jesus exposes this false notion of a compulsory connection between sin and suffering. The Lord's work of healing this man is an exemplary demonstration that all are blind until we come to recognize Jesus as the source of all light.

## Reflection

1. Do you think there is a connection between sickness and sin?

2. Is Jesus just referring to visible light?

3. Why does Jesus tell us "the night is coming, when no one can work"?

## ISAIAH 60:1-3

*Arise, shine, for your light has come, and the glory of the Lord rises upon you. See, darkness covers the earth and thick darkness is over the peoples, but the Lord rises upon you and His glory appears over you. Nations will come to your light, and kings to the brightness of your dawn* (Isaiah 60:1-3).

Isaiah rejoices in the knowledge that the promise of the Lord's coming is fulfilled! The Messiah will scatter the darkness. Even the Gentiles will see His marvelous light. One day the rulers of this world will recognize Him and submit to Him.

## Reflection

1. How is it that we can arise and shine?

2. Is Isaiah telling us that we will recognize the Messiah?

3. Each verse mentions "you" or "your" twice. Who is this "you"?

# Day 20

# The Good Shepherd

## JOHN 10:7-11

*Therefore Jesus said again, "I tell you the truth, I am the gate for the sheep. All who ever came before Me were thieves and robbers, but the sheep did not listen to them. I am the gate; whoever enters through Me will be saved. He will come in and go out, and find pasture. The thief comes only to steal and kill and destroy; I have come that they may have life, and have it to the full.*

*I am the good shepherd. The good shepherd lays down His life for the sheep"* (John 10:7-11).

Jesus explains His relationship with people in terms of being a shepherd. In that day, this example would have been easy to understand. Shepherds protected their sheep by lying down at the entrance to a cave or corral. Jesus uses this analogy as the entry to salvation. Jesus cautions His sheep that there is much to learn about life in this world and about salvation.

## *Reflection*

1.  What does it mean to be a good shepherd?

2.  Why does God use sheep as an example for humans?

3.  What does having "life to the full" look like?

## 1 SAMUEL 16:11-13

*So he asked Jesse, "Are these all the sons you have?"*

*"There is still the youngest," Jesse answered, "but he is tending the sheep."*

*Samuel said, "Send for him; we will not sit down until he arrives." So he sent and had him brought in. He was ruddy, with a fine appearance and handsome features.*

*Then the Lord said, "Rise and anoint him; he is the one."*

*So Samuel took the horn of oil and anointed him in the presence of his brothers, and from that day on the Spirit of the Lord came upon David in power. Samuel then went to Ramah* (1 Samuel 16:11-13).

Samuel came to anoint the next king of Israel. The prophet had reviewed all of Jesse's children except for David, the one least likely to be selected in his father's eyes. Samuel was obedient to God and would not make his choice without all the sons receiving a proper review.

## Reflection

1. What does this event tell you about how God sees His children?

2. How could being a lowly shepherd help David become a king?

3.  What does the anointing oil signify?

4.  What is the connection between David being anointed as king and Jesus, who is the Messiah, which means "the Anointed One"?

# Day 21

## The Resurrection and the Life

### JOHN 11:21-27

*"Lord,"* Martha said to Jesus, *"if You had been here, my brother would not have died. But I know that even now God will give You whatever You ask."*

*Jesus said to her, "Your brother will rise again."*

*Martha answered, "I know he will rise again in the resurrection at the last day."*

*Jesus said to her, "I am the resurrection and the life. He who believes in Me will live, even though he dies; and whoever lives and believes in Me will never die. Do you believe this?"*

*"Yes, Lord," she told Him, "I believe that you are the Christ, the Son of God, who was to come into the world"* (John 11:21-27).

According to Webster's, *resurrection* means "to be returned from the dead, back to life." The ultimate expression of God's sovereignty is that He can take something that is dead and make it live again. Martha tells Him, *"Master, if You had been here, my brother wouldn't have died."* She affirms that God will grant every request of Jesus. Finally, she confirms that Jesus is the Messiah, Ben Elohim, the Anointed One, the Son of God! Amen!

## Reflection

1. How does it make you feel to know that you have eternal life with Christ?

2. Does this change your view of death?

3. Do you realize how important your belief in Jesus is?

4. What do you think you would have said to Jesus if it were your own brother who died?

## 2 SAMUEL 7:12-17

*"When your days are over and you rest with your fathers, I will raise up your offspring to succeed you, who will come from your own body, and I will establish his kingdom. He is the one who will build a house for My Name, and I will establish the throne of his kingdom forever. I will be his father, and he will be My son. When he does wrong, I will punish him with the rod of men, with floggings inflicted by men. But My love will never be taken away from him, as I took it away from Saul, whom I removed from before you. Your house and your kingdom will endure forever before Me; your throne will be established forever."* Nathan reported to David all the words of this entire revelation (2 Samuel 7:12-17).

The Lord told the prophet Nathan to relate these words to King David. King David was shown that, after he died, one of his descendants would establish an everlasting kingdom. This successor would be punished, but God would neither remove His love from Him, nor the heritage of David's throne. This coming king of Israel would be established forever. This promise was fulfilled through Jesus, who was a descendant of David.

## *Reflection*

1. Why would the Lord compare David's reign as king of Israel to Saul's?

2. How much of this promise do you think King David could understand?

# Day 22

## Raised From the Dead

### JOHN 11:39-44

"Take away the stone," He said.

"But, Lord," said Martha, the sister of the dead man, "by this time there is a bad odor, for he has been there four days."

Then Jesus said, "Did I not tell you that if you believed, you would see the glory of God?"

So they took away the stone. Then Jesus looked up and said, "Father, I thank You that You have heard Me. I knew that You always hear Me, but I said this for the benefit of the people standing here, that they may believe that You sent Me."

When He had said this, Jesus called in a loud voice, "Lazarus, come out!" The dead man came out, his hands and feet *wrapped with strips of linen, and a cloth around his face.*

*Jesus said to them, "Take off the grave clothes and let him go"* (John 11:39-44).

Perhaps the most remarkable demonstration of Jesus' authority was His ability to raise the dead. Of all the miracles performed by Jesus, none is more awe-inspiring than the story of Lazarus.

## Reflection

1.  What does it do to your faith to know that God can overcome death?

2.  Is there something in your life that has died that God wants to bring back to life?

3.  Pray about it and see what God can do. (Don't forget to thank Him, too.)

### EZEKIEL 37:3-5

*He asked me, "Son of man, can these bones live?"*

*I said, "O Sovereign Lord, You alone know."*

*Then He said to me, "Prophesy to these bones and say to them, 'Dry bones, hear the word of the Lord! This is what the Sovereign Lord says to these bones: I will make breath enter you, and you will come to life"* (Ezekiel 37:3-5).

It is deeply significant that both the Old and New Testaments speak of resurrection life from death. God's ability to bring life from death has always been available, but He chose Jesus to show us the way. Ezekiel was speaking to a remnant of the nation of Israel that had been exiled and was being held in captivity in Babylon. His words promised life and freedom to a nation that could only see despair.

## Reflection

1. Can you see how God develops a model in the Old Testament to prepare us for His future plan of salvation?

2. How is it that God can plan things many centuries before they take place?

3. Could this represent the restoration of both early and modern-day Israel?

# Day 23

## The Coming King

### JOHN 12:12-16

*The next day the great crowd that had come for the Feast heard that Jesus was on His way to Jerusalem. They took palm branches and went out to meet Him, shouting, "Hosanna!" "Blessed is He who comes in the name of the Lord!" "Blessed is the King of Israel!"*

*Jesus found a young donkey and sat upon it, as it is written, "Do not be afraid, O Daughter of Zion; see, your king is coming, seated on a donkey's colt."*

*At first His disciples did not understand all this. Only after Jesus was glorified did they realize that these things had been written about Him and that they had done these things to Him (John 12:12-16).*

This is the picture of a city welcoming a conquering hero. This was the only time when Jesus allowed Himself to be praised as King. The people of Jerusalem erupted with joy at the news of their coming Ruler.

## Reflection

1. Did Jesus either look like or act like a king?

2. Do you think Jesus expected this response?

3. Why were the people so excited about Jesus' coming?

### ZECHARIAH 9:9-10

*Rejoice greatly, O Daughter of Zion! Shout, Daughter of Jerusalem! See, your king comes to you, righteous and having salvation, gentle and riding on a donkey, on a colt, the foal of a donkey. I will take away the chariots from Ephraim and the war-horses from Jerusalem, and the battle bow will be broken. He will proclaim peace to the nations. His rule will extend from sea to sea and from the River to the ends of the earth* (Zechariah 9:9-10).

This paints the picture of our Lord's coming for us. He was referred to as a king. He was *"righteous and having salvation, gentle and riding on a donkey."* He will speak to all peoples. He will have dominion over all the earth. This verse represents one of more than half a dozen clear prophesies describing the coming Messiah in the Book of Zechariah.

## Reflection

1. Why would Jesus humble Himself to ride a donkey when an animal of stature, like a horse, could have been chosen?

2. What connection do you see between this passage and John 12:15?

3. Do you believe this is a fulfillment of one of God's promises?

# Day 24

## To Everything There Is a Season

### JOHN 12:27-33

*"Now My heart is troubled, and what shall I say? 'Father, save Me from this hour'? No, it was for this very reason I came to this hour. Father, glorify Your name!"*

*Then a voice came from heaven, "I have glorified it, and will glorify it again." The crowd that was there and heard it said it had thundered; others said an angel had spoken to Him.*

*Jesus said, "This voice was for your benefit, not Mine. Now is the time for judgment on this world; now the prince of this world will be driven out. But I, when I am lifted up from the earth, will draw all men to Myself."*

*He said this to show the kind of death He was going to die* (John 12:27-33).

One of the great mysteries of life concerns our beginning (or origin) and our final resting place (or goal). None of us are capable of predicting the experience of either life or death with certainty. Yet Jesus predicted both the time and means of His life and death. God's heavenly masterpiece of perfect timing was set in motion, was walked out on earth, and was ultimately fulfilled on a mount outside the walls of Jerusalem. There, as the ironic symbol of God's triumph through death, is the vision of Jesus being raised high on a cross, suspended between Heaven and earth.

## Reflection

1.  What would you like God to say when you reach the end of your days?

2.  What do you think God wants you to complete during your life?

3.  Has God already shown you His plan?

4.  Are you waiting for His instructions?

## ECCLESIASTES 3:1-2

*There is a time for everything, and a season for every activity under heaven: a time to be born and a time to die, a time to plant and a time to uproot* (Ecclesiastes 3:1-2).

In Ecclesiastes, Solomon, said to be the wisest man who ever lived, attempted to pull together the loose ends of his life into an understandable context. As we gain this king's perspective on life, we see God's perfect timing, even in the midst of seemingly random circumstances. Solomon finally concluded that, apart from the revelation of knowing God, life has no meaning or significance (see Eccles. 2:24-26).

## *Reflection*

1.  Does this passage give you a broader understanding of the seasons of your life?

2.  Do you think fulfilling God's plan for your life will affect your encounter with Him after you die?

# Day 25

## Sitting at His Feet

### JOHN 13:3-9

*Jesus knew that the Father had put all things under His power, and that He had come from God and was returning to God; so He got up from the meal, took off His outer clothing, and wrapped a towel around His waist. After that, He poured water into a basin and began to wash His disciples' feet, drying them with the towel that was wrapped around Him.*

*He came to Simon Peter, who said to Him, "Lord, are You going to wash my feet?"*

*Jesus replied, "You do not realize now what I am doing, but later you will understand."*

*"No," said Peter, "You shall never wash my feet."*

*Jesus answered, "Unless I wash you, you have no part with Me."*

*"Then, Lord," Simon Peter replied, "not just my feet but my hands and my head as well"* (John 13:3-9).

The feet of a traveler were always dirty—road grime, animal waste, and mud. To wash a person's feet was a lowly task, set aside for the least-respected member of a household. Imagine the embarrassment of Peter when Jesus, the one he revered, the one who was presiding over the Passover feast, knelt before him in the most humble posture.

## Reflection

1. Have you thought about the price Jesus had to pay to wash you clean?

2. Are there parts of your life that you don't want anyone to see?

3. Are you willing to give all your shame, pain, and pride to Jesus?

## RUTH 3:3-7

*Wash and perfume yourself, and put on your best clothes. Then go down to the threshing floor, but don't let him know you are there until he has finished eating and drinking. When he lies down, note the place where he is lying. Then go and uncover his feet and lie down. He will tell you what to do."*

*"I will do whatever you say," Ruth answered. So she went down to the threshing floor and did everything her mother-in-law told her to do.*

*When Boaz had finished eating and drinking and was in good spirits, he went over to lie down at the far end of the grain pile. Ruth approached quietly, uncovered his feet and lay down* (Ruth 3:3-7).

Ruth was a Moabite, not a Hebrew. She took her place at the feet of a landowner, a man of high standing in the city. He could have rejected her and swept her away, and no one would have thought twice about it. Yet Boaz accepted her and loved her. Their union spawned the heritage of King David. Yes, that's right. Because of the humility of a Gentile and the generosity of a Jew, royalty came to earth. Glory to God!

## Reflection

1. How hard is it for you to humble yourself before others?

2. How does seeing our royal heritage affect your view of God?

3. Is there anything that God hasn't done to prove His love to you?

# Day 26

## That You Love One Another

### JOHN 13:33-35

*My children, I will be with you only a little longer. You will look for Me, and just as I told the Jews, so I tell you now: Where I am going, you cannot come. A new command I give you: Love one another. As I have loved you, so you must love one another. By this all men will know that you are My disciples, if you love one another* (John 13:33-35).

Jesus was going to leave the earth to return to Heaven, and He had some last words—a commandment! He told His disciples that the world would recognize His life in us by our love. Only God can give commandments to humanity. This is His instruction—that we love one another. Awesome.

# Reflection

1. What does this commandment tell you about the person of Jesus?

2. How does this commandment compare to the original Ten Commandments found in Exodus 20?

3. How does this change your perspective on love?

## MICAH 6:8

. . . . . . . . . . . . . . . . . . . . . . . . .

*He has showed you, O man, what is good. And what does the Lord require of you? To act justly and to love mercy and to walk humbly with your God (Micah 6:8).*

In a complicated world with so many ideas about spirituality, here is a simple statement about what God expects of us. The Lord reminds us that He has demonstrated what is good. Now He is asking us to live our lives with fairness, compassion, and humility. He is not a God who is harsh or vindictive, but a God who loves us. Joy!

## *Reflection*

1. What can God do with a person who offers his/her all to Him?

2. Has the Lord set the bar too high for us to reach?

3. Do you think God understands us?

# Day 27

## Preparing a Place for You

### JOHN 14:1-6

*"Do not let your hearts be troubled. Trust in God; trust also in Me. In My Father's house are many rooms; if it were not so, I would have told you. I am going there to prepare a place for you. And if I go and prepare a place for you, I will come back and take you to be with Me that you also may be where I am. You know the way to the place where I am going."*

*Thomas said to Him, "Lord, we don't know where You are going, so how can we know the way?"*

*Jesus answered, "I am the way and the truth and the life. No one comes to the Father except through Me"* (John 14:1-6).

In life, it is very difficult to stay on the right path and to know who you can trust. How remarkable it is to discover in Jesus the absolute truth. May we ever be grateful that God has made His person and His way known to us through the life of His Son.

## Reflection

1. Have you ever met anyone who knows the way, the truth, and the life?

2. Why should you trust Jesus to be the answer to these questions?

3. How does a person find Father God?

## 1 CHRONICLES 17:11-14

*When your days are over and you go to be with your fathers, I will raise up your offspring to succeed you, one of your own sons, and I will establish his kingdom. He is the one who will build a house for Me, and I will establish his throne forever. I*

*will be his Father, and he will be My son.
I will never take My love away from him,
as I took it away from your predecessor.
I will set him over My house and My
kingdom forever; his throne will be established forever* (1 Chronicles 17:11-14).

What a great comfort to know that, after we have died, future generations will carry on the work that we have begun during our brief time here. We are part of something much bigger than our individual lives. Our family can continue to build the Kingdom of God. May they know the truth that God has revealed to us through Jesus.

## Reflection

1.  Is having a godly heritage something you have ever considered?

2.  How well do you know the history of your family?

3.  What do you hope for the coming generations of your family?

# Day 28

## Abiding in God's House

### JOHN 15:1-5

*I am the true vine, and My Father is the gardener. He cuts off every branch in Me that bears no fruit, while every branch that does bear fruit He prunes so that it will be even more fruitful. You are already clean because of the word I have spoken to you. Remain in Me, and I will remain in you. No branch can bear fruit by itself; it must remain in the vine. Neither can you bear fruit unless you remain in Me.*

*I am the vine; you are the branches. If a man remains in Me and I in him, he will bear much fruit; apart from Me you can do nothing (John 15:1-5).*

Jesus illustrates the relationship between Himself and His heavenly Father as He explains the nature of His relationship to us. We are called to abide with the one who makes us fruitful. As with the branch and the vine, this connection is vital; it provides sustenance and yields abundance through His empowering.

## Reflection

1. Do things that are not fruitful often frustrate you?

2. Do you believe that doing things that honor Jesus will succeed?

3. How does this change the course of your life?

### EZRA 3:10-11

*When the builders laid the foundation of the temple of the Lord, the priests in their vestments and with trumpets, and the Levites (the sons of Asaph) with cymbals, took their places to praise the Lord, as prescribed by David king of Israel. With praise and thanksgiving they sang to the Lord:*

*"He is good; His love to Israel endures forever."*

*And all the people gave a great shout of praise to the Lord, because the foundation of the house of the Lord was laid* (Ezra 3:10-11).

By the grace of God, the Temple that had been destroyed was being rebuilt. A great celebration took place. The house that represented Israel's relationship with their Creator had its cornerstone laid. The divine plan of redemption was underway, with God undergirding Israel's foundation.

## Reflection

1.  How does it feel to accomplish something bigger than you?

2. Are you joyful when you are doing things for God?

3. Does God need a house as much as you do?

# Day 29

## The Reason for Love

### JOHN 15:9-13

*As the Father has loved Me, so have I loved you. Now remain in My love. If you obey My commands, you will remain in My love, just as I have obeyed My Father's commands and remain in His love. I have told you this so that My joy may be in you and that your joy may be complete. My command is this: Love each other as I have loved you. Greater love has no one than this, that he lay down his life for his friends* (John 15:9-13).

We often talk about love. We seldom look at what God calls love. Biblical love requires a sacrifice. For God to love us cost Him the life of His Son. Yet that was the Lord's reason for being here—to lay down His life for us.

## Reflection

1. How does God's love compare to ours?

2. Have you ever loved someone so much you would die for him or her?

### PROVERBS 10:12

. . . . . . . . . . . . . . . . . . . . . . . . . . . . .

*Hatred stirs up dissension, but love covers over all wrongs* (Proverbs 10:12).

Consider how much time you spend learning about and thinking about love. Usually this is in the context of your relationships with your fellow human beings. Looking at your relationship with God requires a different perspective. Try to imagine what God thinks about love.

## Reflection

1. What do you think God feels about you?

2. Is it hard to think about God loving you?

3. How can love cover all sins?

# Day 30

# Dealing With Rejection

## JOHN 15:18-25

*If the world hates you, keep in mind that it hated Me first. If you belonged to the world, it would love you as its own. As it is, you do not belong to the world, but I have chosen you out of the world. That is why the world hates you. Remember the words I spoke to you: "No servant is greater than his master." If they persecuted Me, they will persecute you also. If they obeyed My teaching, they will obey yours also. They will treat you this way because of My name, for they do not know the One who sent Me. If I had not come and spoken to them, they would not be guilty of sin. Now, however, they have no excuse for their sin. He who hates Me hates My Father as well. If I had not done among them what no one else did, they would not be guilty of sin. But now they have seen these miracles, and yet they have hated both Me and My Father. But this is to fulfill what is written in their Law: "They hated Me without reason"* (John 15:18-25).

B eing a leader is not always a popular position. Sometimes it is necessary to counter beliefs that are leading people down the wrong path. This often leads to rejection of that leader. The best example in history is this of Jesus. The ones He came to help demanded His crucifixion.

## Reflection

1. Have you ever had to stand for an unpopular belief?

2. How does it feel to be rejected?

3. What do you think is the cause of hatred?

## NEHEMIAH 2:15-20

So I went up the valley by night, examining the wall. Finally, I turned back and reentered through the Valley Gate. The officials did not know where I had gone or what I was doing, because as yet I had said nothing to the Jews or the priests or nobles or officials or any others who would be doing the work.

Then I said to them, "You see the trouble we are in: Jerusalem lies in ruins, and its gates have been burned with fire. Come, let us rebuild the wall of Jerusalem, and we will no longer be in disgrace." I also told them about the gracious hand of my God upon me and what the king had said to me.

They replied, "Let us start rebuilding." So they began this good work.

But when Sanballat the Horonite, Tobiah the Ammonite official and Geshem the Arab heard about it, they mocked and ridiculed us. "What is this you are doing?"

*they asked. "Are you rebelling against the king?"*

*I answered them by saying, "The God of heaven will give us success. We His servants will start rebuilding, but as for you, you have no share in Jerusalem or any claim or historic right to it"* (Nehemiah 2:15-20).

Often times a leader has to look into situations that require a new approach and a strong hand. Nehemiah didn't even tell his Hebrew compatriots that he was going to inspect the broken walls. Ironically, the leader of many had to spend time alone to hear from God and assess his situation. Nehemiah knew the ways of his enemies.

## Reflection

1. What is the advantage of discovering things for yourself?

2. Are you often surprised when you encounter resistance?

# Day 31

## Getting Upset With God

### JOHN 16:5-11

*Now I am going to Him who sent Me, yet none of you asks Me, "Where are You going?" Because I have said these things, you are filled with grief. But I tell you the truth: It is for your good that I am going away. Unless I go away, the Counselor will not come to you; but if I go, I will send Him to you. When He comes, He will convict the world of guilt in regard to sin and righteousness and judgment: in regard to sin, because men do not believe in Me; in regard to righteousness, because I am going to the Father, where you can see Me no longer; and in regard to judgment, because the prince of this world now stands condemned (John 16:5-11).*

Jesus had the difficult task of telling His disciples that it was time for Him to go. He knew that this would bring them much sorrow, but He also knew that the Helper (the Holy Spirit) would not come unless He left.

After the Helper comes, the time of judgment begins. This is not a popular concept for us to accept. However, the Lord is serious about His calling upon our lives. The Good News is that we can be encouraged because we have a Helper, a Comforter, and an Advocate on our behalf, and that is the Lord Jesus.

## *Reflection*

1. Do you get upset when someone you love goes away?

2. Are you reassured to know that they will return?

3. How does it make you feel to know that Jesus has sent the Holy Spirit?

4. Does it disturb you that the world comes under God's judgment?

## ZEPHANIAH 2:1-2

......................................................

*Gather together, gather together, O shameful nation, before the appointed time arrives and that day sweeps on like chaff, before the fierce anger of the Lord comes upon you, before the day of the Lord's wrath comes upon you* (Zephaniah 2:1-2).

This passage of Zephaniah is a call to the nation of Israel to come together in an assembly to pray, to repent, and to humble themselves before God. Sometimes in the Bible we see and hear of God's fierce anger and coming judgment. God was just as upset with sin in those days as He is now. But today we have a relationship with God because of the work that Jesus did on the cross to separate those who believe in Him from the power of sin. Thank God!

## Reflection

1. Why would God not desire a nation?

2. Was God's judgment in the day of Zephaniah different than God's judgment today?

3. What difference does our relationship with the Holy Spirit make in regard to God's judgment upon humanity?

4. Is it acceptable for us to be upset with God?

# Day 32

## Tribulation

### JOHN 16:32-33

*But a time is coming, and has come, when you will be scattered, each to his own home. You will leave Me all alone. Yet I am not alone, for My Father is with Me. I have told you these things, so that in Me you may have peace. In this world you will have trouble. But take heart! I have overcome the world* (John 16:32-33).

As much protection as God gives His children, there is no way to avoid the tribulation that comes from living in this world. Jesus doesn't tell us that our walk with Him is always safe. Instead, He tells us that He has overcome every battle that we ever have faced or ever will face. The Lord is telling us that having faith in Him means we can defeat every enemy. Glory!

# Reflection

1. Is it difficult for you to put your faith in God?

2. Why would God allow the world to have so much suffering?

3. Is it necessary for us to overcome the world?

## JOB 40:2-5

*"Will the one who contends with the Almighty correct Him? Let him who accuses God answer Him!"*

*Then Job answered the Lord: "I am unworthy—how can I reply to You? I put my hand over my mouth. I spoke once, but I have no answer—twice, but I will say no more"* (Job 40:2-5).

Job knew it was futile trying to argue with the one who has every answer. Job was afflicted. Everything that Job valued was taken away. The Lord knows why we have trouble. He has allowed our troubles for a purpose higher than we can contemplate. Anyone who has disagreed with God soon discovers that there is no winning such an argument.

## *Reflection*

1.  What is the benefit of arguing?

2.  Are you willing to accept an answer that disagrees with your own?

3.  Aren't there times when you must correct a loved one? Or a foe?

4.  How do you face tribulation?

# Day 33

## God's Highest Calling

*My prayer is not for them alone. I pray also for those who will believe in Me through their message, that all of them may be one, Father, just as You are in Me and I am in You. May they also be in Us so that the world may believe that You have sent Me. I have given them the glory that You gave Me, that they may be one as We are one: I in them and You in Me. May they be brought to complete unity to let the world know that You sent Me and have loved them even as You have loved Me (John 17:20-23).*

For many, these prayers represent the pinnacle of Christ's ministry. Jesus said that He had been glorified and that He wants us to be glorified as well. He went even farther by declaring that this is the reason why He came—that is, that we would be united in love as one with God forever. This was His highest calling. This is what Jesus died for. Amen.

## Reflection

1.  Consider the prayers of Jesus and ask yourself, "Is there anything greater than this that the Lord could do for me?"

2.  How important is it to you to know the purpose for your life?

3.  Are you looking forward to being glorified with God?

### ESTHER 4:12-14

*When Esther's words were reported to Mordecai, he sent back this answer: "Do not think that because you are in the king's house you alone of all the Jews will escape. For if you remain silent at this time, relief and deliverance for the Jews will arise from another place, but you and your father's family will perish. And who knows but that you have come to royal position for such a time as this?"* (Esther 4:12-14)

Queen Esther had favor as the wife of a king. Yet even with her exalted position, she could not approach the king without a specific invitation from him. In this passage, Esther was being encouraged to approach the king without such an invitation. This decision could be cause for an immediate death sentence. But Esther decided to overcome her fear of dying because she knew the reason she had been placed in the royal court.

## Reflection

1.  How does it affect you to know that a person is willing to die for what he or she believes?

2.  In fact, are we not all living out our beliefs?

3. Jesus and Esther were willing to die for what they believed. Are you?

# Day 34

## Betrayal

### JOHN 18:4-6

*Jesus, knowing all that was going to happen to Him, went out and asked them, "Who is it you want?"*

*"Jesus of Nazareth," they replied.*

*"I am He," Jesus said. (And Judas the traitor was standing there with them.) When Jesus said, "I am He," they drew back and fell to the ground (John 18:4-6).*

In the Garden of Gethsemane, Judas, the disciple who had betrayed Jesus, confronted Him. He was accompanied by a large group of armed temple guards. When Jesus responded to them, they all were knocked to the ground by a supernatural force. Certainly Jesus knew Judas would betray Him, as He had forewarned the disciples earlier in the evening at the Passover Seder in the upper room.

## Reflection

1. Have you ever been betrayed by someone you cared for?

2. Do you think Jesus could have prevented His capture?

3. What power was Jesus drawing upon when the armed guards were sent backward?

4. Did Jesus go willingly to the cross?

### JUDGES 16:18-21

*When Delilah saw that he had told her everything, she sent word to the rulers of the Philistines, "Come back once more; he has told me everything." So the rulers of the Philistines returned with the silver in their hands. Having put him to sleep on her lap, she called a man to shave off the seven braids of his hair, and so began to subdue him. And his strength left him.*

*Then she called, "Samson, the Philistines are upon you!"*

*He awoke from his sleep and thought, "I'll go out as before and shake myself free." But he did not know that the Lord had left him.*

*Then the Philistines seized him, gouged out his eyes and took him down to Gaza. Binding him with bronze shackles, they set him to grinding in the prison* (Judges 16:18-21).

The story of Samson and Delilah culminates in Delilah's discovery of the source of Samson's strength—his hair. Upon having his head shaved, Samson lost his strength, but he did not realize that the presence of the Lord had departed from him. Thus, he was taken captive.

## Reflection

1. Did Samson go willingly to his capture?

2. What can we learn from Samson's revealing of the source of his power to a person whom he could not trust?

3. Why would God allow someone he loves to be betrayed?

# Day 35

## Judging the World

### JOHN 18:33-36

*Pilate then went back inside the palace, summoned Jesus and asked Him, "Are You the king of the Jews?"*

*"Is that your own idea," Jesus asked, "or did others talk to you about Me?"*

*"Am I a Jew?" Pilate replied. "It was Your people and Your chief priests who handed You over to me. What is it You have done?"*

*Jesus said, "My kingdom is not of this world. If it were, My servants would fight to prevent My arrest by the Jews. But now My kingdom is from another place"* (John 18:33-36).

Jesus was cross-examined by a very curious Pontius Pilate. The Roman Curator was amazed by the response he got. Jesus told him, *"My king-dom is not of this world...."* Jesus knew that the day will come when the scepter of judgment will change hands. Although Pilate had the power to sentence Jesus to death, Jesus' comment must have frightened the governor.

## Reflection

1.  Have you ever been asked to determine someone's guilt or innocence?

2.  What questions would you ask Jesus if you could?

3.  Do you think our Lord will ask you questions when you finally meet Him face-to-face?

### NAHUM 1:2-5

*The Lord is a jealous and avenging God; the Lord takes vengeance and is filled with wrath. The Lord takes vengeance on His foes and maintains His wrath against His enemies. The Lord is slow to anger and great in power; the Lord will not leave the guilty unpunished. His way is in the whirlwind and the storm, and clouds are the dust of His feet. He rebukes the sea and dries it up; He makes all the rivers run dry. Bashan and Carmel wither and the blossoms of Lebanon fade. The mountains quake before Him and the hills melt away. The earth trembles at His presence, the world and all who live in it* (Nahum 1:2-5).

These verses reveal an all-powerful God who is more than capable of passing judgment and changing the course of our lives in an instant. How fortunate we are that the Lord is slow to anger, but will avenge those in need of protection. Imagine having that much power and authority. Let us be thankful that the Lord chooses mercy before judgment.

## Reflection

1. How would you behave if you had that much power?

2. How do you respond to seeing the depths of God's authority?

3. Do you think this is the primary perspective many have of God? Why?

# Day 36

# Prophecy Fulfilled

### JOHN 19:17-19, 23-24

*Carrying His own cross, He went out to the place of the Skull (which in Aramaic is called Golgotha). Here they crucified Him, and with Him two others—one on each side and Jesus in the middle.*

*Pilate had a notice prepared and fastened to the cross. It read: JESUS OF NAZARETH, THE KING OF THE JEWS.*

*…When the soldiers crucified Jesus, they took His clothes, dividing them into four shares, one for each of them, with the undergarment remaining. This garment was seamless, woven in one piece from top to bottom.*

*"Let's not tear it," they said to one another. "Let's decide by lot who will get it."*

*This happened that the scripture might be fulfilled that said, "They divided my clothes among them and cast lots for my garment." So this is what the soldiers did (John 19:17-19, 23-24).*

John draws the image of Christ's crucifixion with clarity and detail. The accuracy of this telling verifies the Word of God. Let us marvel at the intricacy of God's design as every facet is revealed. Imagine all the unwitting players He used to orchestrate this pathway to glorify His Son. The blood sacrifice of Jesus is the defining chronicle of God's plan of redemption. May we always hold these proceedings with reverence.

## Reflection

1. In what ways do you see the intentionality of God in this setting?

2. How does the crucifixion story include profiles of those who were witnesses and participants in the death of Christ?

3. Why are these witnesses important?

## PSALM 22:14-18

*I am poured out like water, and all my bones are out of joint. My heart has turned to wax; it has melted away within me.*

*My strength is dried up like a potsherd, and my tongue sticks to the roof of my mouth; you lay me in the dust of death.*

*Dogs have surrounded me; a band of evil men has encircled me, they have pierced my hands and my feet.*

*I can count all my bones; people stare and gloat over me.*

*They divide my garments among them and cast lots for my clothing* (Psalm 22:14-18).

King David penned these words under the divine inspiration of the Holy Spirit. Psalm 22 contains numerous clear prophetic pictures of Jesus' crucifixion. After 1,000 years, the psalm given to Israel's King was reenacted—with each element falling exactly into place. Amazing!

# *Reflection*

1. Can you sense the anguish of our Lord's death in this psalm?

2. Why do you think the Messiah had to suffer?

3. In what ways does this scene represent the surrender of all physical possessions?

# Day 37

## It Is Finished

*Later, knowing that all was now completed, and so that the Scripture would be fulfilled, Jesus said, "I am thirsty." A jar of wine vinegar was there, so they soaked a sponge in it, put the sponge on a stalk of the hyssop plant, and lifted it to Jesus' lips. When He had received the drink, Jesus said, "It is finished." With that, He bowed His head and gave up His spirit* (John 19:28-30).

The glory of the death of Jesus is very understated. The Holy Scriptures tell us some of what was done to Him, but it includes very few words about the anguish of His suffering. Jesus knew that He had finished the work He came to accomplish. Having done all, He gave up His spirit.

## *Reflection*

1. Do you think Jesus decided when He was going to die?

2. How would Jesus know He had finished His work here?

3. Hyssop was used to smear the blood of the Passover Lamb onto the doorways of Israelite homes before their Exodus from Egypt. Do you see any patterns emerging here?

### ISAIAH 53:4-5

*Surely He took up our infirmities and carried our sorrows, yet we considered Him stricken by God, smitten by Him, and afflicted.*

*But He was pierced for our transgressions, He was crushed for our iniquities;*

*the punishment that brought us peace was upon Him, and by His wounds we are healed* (Isaiah 53:4-5).

These words point to a person who was willing to suffer for the benefit of others. It is clear that a substitution has been made so that others would be healed.

## Reflection

1. Does this individual sound like Jesus?

2. Is this consistent with God's plan of redemption for sin?

3. Can one man make this much difference in the Kingdom of God?

# Day 38

## Our Redeemer Lives

JOHN 20:5-9

*He bent over and looked in at the strips of linen lying there but did not go in. Then Simon Peter, who was behind him, arrived and went into the tomb. He saw the strips of linen lying there, as well as the burial cloth that had been around Jesus' head. The cloth was folded up by itself, separate from the linen. Finally the other disciple, who had reached the tomb first, also went inside. He saw and believed. (They still did not understand from Scripture that Jesus had to rise from the dead) (John 20:5-9).*

They looked inside the tomb where their master had been laid to rest, but no body could be found. They found only the remnants of

His burial linens and the handkerchief that had covered His face. Interestingly, it was carefully folded. But there was not a trace of Jesus.

## Reflection

1. Where would someone hide the body? Was this a hoax?

2. Why would someone remove the body from the burial linens?

3. Why do you think the disciples did not recall Jesus' words that He would rise from the dead?

### HOSEA 13:14A

*I will ransom them from the power of the grave; I will redeem them from death* (Hosea 13:14a).

God is not afraid of death. In fact, the realm of Heaven has been prepared for our death. The Holy Spirit challenges our whole idea of beginnings and endings. With God, the whole purpose of the boundaries of life and death requires a new vision into the spiritual dimension. There is a place we call Heaven, and it is the place where we will spend our eternity because death was conquered by Jesus on the cross. Rejoice!

## *Reflection*

1. Do you enjoy reading about death being conquered?

2. Why would God need to ransom somebody?

3. Do you think this talk about death is exaggerated?

# Day 39

## Holy Spirit With Us

### JOHN 20:19-23

On the evening of that first day of the week, when the disciples were together, with the doors locked for fear of the Jews, Jesus came and stood among them and said, "Peace be with you!" After He said this, He showed them His hands and side. The disciples were overjoyed when they saw the Lord.

Again Jesus said, "Peace be with you! As the Father has sent Me, I am sending you." And with that He breathed on them and said, "Receive the Holy Spirit. If you forgive anyone his sins, they are forgiven; if you do not forgive them, they are not forgiven" (John 20:19-23).

After Jesus died and was entombed, His body disappeared. The disciples continued to gather together to pray, but none were prepared for an actual appearance of their Lord. Jesus not only appeared to them, but also showed them the places where His body had been pierced. He spoke and bid them, *"Peace be with you."* Then He breathed on them and imparted the gift of the Holy Spirit. Resurrection power!

## Reflection

1. How would you have responded in the upper room that night?

2. How significant is it that Jesus returned in bodily form?

3. What does receiving the gift of the Holy Spirit mean to you personally?

## HAGGAI 2:4-9

*"But now be strong, O Zerubbabel,"* declares the Lord. *"Be strong, O Joshua*

*son of Jehozadak, the high priest. Be strong, all you people of the land," declares the Lord, "and work. For I am with you," declares the Lord Almighty. "This is what I covenanted with you when you came out of Egypt. And My Spirit remains among you. Do not fear."*

*This is what the Lord Almighty says: "In a little while I will once more shake the heavens and the earth, the sea and the dry land. I will shake all nations, and the desired of all nations will come, and I will fill this house with glory," says the Lord Almighty. "The silver is Mine and the gold is Mine," declares the Lord Almighty. "The glory of this present house will be greater than the glory of the former house," says the Lord Almighty. "And in this place I will grant peace," declares the Lord Almighty* (Haggai 2:4-9).

In the Book of Haggai, we see a preview of God's desire that His Spirit remain with His children. This book was written while the temple in Jerusalem was being rebuilt. Although this temple was not as magnificent as the original temple constructed by Solomon, God promised that this latter temple would exhibit even more of His glory than the first. God determined that His Spirit would remain with His people.

## *Reflection*

1. How does this latter temple relate to the temple of our human bodies? (See First Corinthians 6:19.)

2. Has it always been God's plan that His Spirit would remain?

3. What difference does the continuing presence of the Holy Spirit make for us?

# Day 40

## God's Great Mercy

### JOHN 21:15-17

*When they had finished eating, Jesus said to Simon Peter, "Simon son of John, do you truly love Me more than these?"*

*"Yes, Lord," he said, "You know that I love You."*

*Jesus said, "Feed My lambs."*

*Again Jesus said, "Simon son of John, do you truly love Me?"*

*He answered, "Yes, Lord, You know that I love You."*

*Jesus said, "Take care of My sheep."*

*The third time He said to him, "Simon son of John, do you love Me?"*

*Peter was hurt because Jesus asked him the third time, "Do you love Me?" He said,*

*"Lord, You know all things; You know that I love You."*

*Jesus said, "Feed My sheep* (John 21:15-17).

Before Jesus ascended into Heaven, He restored all of His relationships with His remaining disciples. Jesus paid particular attention to Simon Peter, who had denied knowing Him three times on the night that our Lord was taken captive.

## Reflection

1. Has God begun His restoration work in you?

2. In what ways is the Lord changing you?

3. What does it mean to you, knowing that God wants to fully restore you?

## LAMENTATIONS 3:22-26

*Because of the Lord's great love we are not consumed, for His compassions never fail. They are new every morning; great is Your faithfulness. I say to myself, "The Lord is my portion; therefore I will wait for Him."*

*The Lord is good to those whose hope is in Him, to the one who seeks Him; it is good to wait quietly for the salvation of the Lord. It is good that one should hope and wait quietly for the salvation of the Lord* (Lamentations 3:22-26).

The Book of Lamentations causes us to look directly at the result of our disobedience in sin. To *lament* is to feel deep anguish at having offended God. Without a genuine sense of remorse, we will fail to recognize how profoundly our actions affect the heart of God Himself. These dynamic verses give us a fresh ray of hope and remind us that our God is merciful. No matter how grievous our error, He is always ready to receive us in His arms of love. Amen.

# Reflection

1. How important is it that the Lord offers mercy before judgment?

2. How does this passage help us to build our faith in Him, knowing that He is faithful to us?

3. Think about how Jesus became the image of God's mercy for us.

# Continuing Your Walk
## with the Lord

Now that you have had the opportunity to *"taste and see that the Lord is good"* (Ps. 34:8), be encouraged to continue studying the Word of God on a daily basis.

A steady diet of the Holy Scriptures is the best way to maintain a healthy, joyous, rewarding walk with the Lord. His Word is life and you have just sipped from the fountain that sustains you for eternity.

Studying the Bible builds confidence that these are God's divinely inspired words. This pursuit teaches one to hear and recognize His voice. Let this be the beginning of a lifelong pursuit to "draw near to God as He draws near to you" (see James 4:8 NKJV).

Knowing God's Word is knowing God's heart. Such wisdom grants one revelation of truth and divine favor. The Word of God is a sure path that never fails.

As your faith grows, seek the company of fellow believers. Pray, praise, and worship God. Make your time with Him your highest priority.

May your walk with the Lord be the light that draws many to faith in God.

> *The Lord bless you and keep you; the Lord make His face shine upon you, and be gracious to you; the Lord lift up His countenance upon you, and give you peace* (Numbers 6:24-26 NKJV).

Myfirst40days.com

# Appendix A

# Old Testament Summary

**Genesis:** Genesis tells the story of God's creation of the heavens and the earth. Beginning with Adam and Eve, God populated the planet. However, they sinned and were banished from the Garden of Eden. Humanity grew and sin spread, so God decided to flood the earth, saving only Noah and his family. One of Noah's descendants, Abraham, was called forward as God's example of faith. His offspring set the stage for a nation to become God's chosen people.

**Exodus:** Exodus tells of how Abraham's offspring had multiplied over four centuries of servitude in Egypt. God then chose Moses to release plagues of judgment on the Egyptians and to lead Israel from Egypt to the Promised Land. On the way, He gave them the Torah (the first five books of the Old Testament) and instructions for living as followers of God.

**Leviticus:** Leviticus gives priestly instructions for overseeing the nation of Israel in both spiritual and daily life. The teachings emphasize worship, obedience, sacrifice, and holiness.

**Numbers:** Numbers covers the time of Israel's wanderings through the wilderness for 40 years. We experience the lessons and complaining of Israel in the midst of God's protective covering over His children as they are prepared to enter the Promised Land.

**Deuteronomy:** Deuteronomy recounts numerous discourses by Moses as he prepares the Israelites to be obedient to God. Moses emphasized the proper posture of gratefulness in living a life of dedication to the Lord.

**Joshua:** This book tells the story of Joshua, the successor of Moses. It details the overcoming of the adversaries of Israel, who had not honored God and were routed out of Canaan, the Promised Land.

**Judges:** Judges covers Israel's history after Joshua, as they repeatedly rebelled against God, suffered from enemies, repented, and called out for judges (champions) to deliver them and restore a right relationship with God.

**Ruth:** Ruth tells the story of a widowed daughter-in-law of a Jewish woman who returned to Israel to serve her bereaved mother. Through obedience and service, Ruth was fully restored.

**First Samuel:** First Samuel begins the review of Israel's history by relating the nation's rejection of God in favor of appointing a king. Despite clear warnings from the prophet Samuel, their first king, Saul, began strong, but was unable to maintain godly standards of leadership.

**Second Samuel:** Second Samuel shows David anointed as king. He desired to build a kingdom that would reflect God's glory here on earth. He spent most of his life uniting the tribes of Israel and conquering their foes. Late in life, his lack of restraint and selfishness put his nation at risk.

**First Kings:** First Kings covers the career of King Solomon, who led a united Israel for 40 peaceful years. Israel achieved greatness and built a magnificent temple, displaying God's glory and favor. Yet Solomon's successes gradually dissipated, and Israel returned to a divided state.

**Second Kings:** Second Kings begins as the prophet Elijah ascends to Heaven and hands his mantle to Elisha. Here is the history of numerous additional kings in both Israel (north) and Judah (south). These two kingdoms were often disobedient and at odds with each other, and the book traces their separate paths to tragic endings. Eventually both regions were conquered and led into captivity.

**First Chronicles:** First Chronicles recounts the history of David's family and reviews the significant events of the kingdom of Israel's past. More than a retelling of history, this book (and Second Chronicles) focuses on the moral and prophetic aspects of spiritual and priestly leadership.

**Second Chronicles:** Second Chronicles contrasts the lessons of good and evil kings. There is a clear delineation between the obedience that led to salvation and the indifference or rebellion that led to destruction. Focusing on the southern kingdom, Judah, the book spans 400 years from the building of the first temple to the edict to build the second temple.

**Ezra:** Ezra had returned to Israel because the Temple had been torn down. He gathered builders and craftsmen together to restore the house of God. After 70 years of captivity, he led the first contingent of Jews back to their homeland to commence work.

**Nehemiah:** The Book of Nehemiah completes the review of Old Testament history. Starting with the remarkably swift reconstruction of the walls of Jerusalem, Nehemiah oversaw the rebuilding of the temple and renewal of Israel under the disapproving gaze of local officials.

**Esther:** Esther is the story of God's favor on a queen who risked her life to protect her Jewish constituents across the known world. Despite the plotting of a villainous magistrate, she exposed his manipulations and delivered her people from sure destruction.

**Job:** Job is the oldest story in the Holy Scriptures. A devout man who had achieved renowned success, Job was sorely tested without any understanding of the cause of such painful treatment.

After suffering multiple onslaughts, he refused to give up on God and was vindicated.

**Psalms:** Psalms is a stunning collection of Hebrew poetry and songs spanning the depth of human experience. A variety of lyrics divulging praise, sorrow, battles, judgment, peace, prophecy, and so forth combine to search our souls for some understanding of God's complexity.

**Proverbs:** Proverbs tells of God's unending wisdom. Jewels of knowledge are scattered across every page. Introspection on the human condition reveals our strengths and weaknesses. Pitfalls to destruction are uncovered. Paths of righteousness are exalted.

**Ecclesiastes:** Ecclesiastes compiles the wisdom of King Solomon. After plentiful living, we discover the vanity we strive for carries little or no value. The only thing that will last is our relationship with God and our obedience to fulfill His call upon our lives.

**Song of Solomon:** Song of Solomon is the love song of the Bible. God tells of His immeasurable love for His creation as we witness the fervent passion a husband and wife feel for one another.

**Isaiah:** The Book of Isaiah begins the books of the prophets. Isaiah foretells the birth, death, and resurrection of the coming Messiah in numerous passages. He gives voice to the Lord's warnings that Israel's sins must be addressed or God will judge His people.

**Jeremiah:** Jeremiah, referred to as the crying prophet, poured out his heart for an Israel that refused to listen to God's instructions and repent. Despite being rejected, Jeremiah continued to alert his fellow countrymen that God would remove the people from their homeland.

**Lamentations:** Lamentations utters our Lord's sorrow over the nation of Israel's sin. We hear the heart of God as He suffers over the funeral of a city. Penned by Jeremiah, this book tells Israel that they are going to pay a great price for their rebellion, yet recognizes the victory to come.

**Ezekiel:** Ezekiel spoke to the exiled Israelites in utter despair. He reminded them of the dire consequences for not repenting, even when they were held captive. He prophesied future battles and the glorious salvation of Israel. His prophetic words to Israel continue to find application in our contemporary world.

**Daniel:** Daniel stood strong despite the opposition that surrounded him and his compatriots. He refused to submit to the forces of foreign governments to control his life or his steadfast worship of God, even at the peril of his own life. The Lord gave him stunning victories.

**Hosea:** Hosea was called to demonstrate God's unwavering desire to forgive even the most hardened of sinners. Hosea's wife would not honor her marriage vows. However, despite her disgraceful behavior, the Lord had Hosea forgive her grievous misdeeds and redeem her.

**Joel:** Joel spoke of the coming Day of the Lord. This future day will be harsher than anything we have ever experienced, but Almighty God will bless His faithful ones. Joel reminded Israel that the Lord has mercy for those who will turn from their sin and return to the Lord.

**Amos:** Amos spoke to those who offered sacrifices and pretended to have pure motives, but lacked righteousness and an understanding of the nature of God. Though Israel was prospering, there was hypocrisy. Impure sacrifices would not deter the Lord's insistence on righteousness.

**Obadiah:** Obadiah warned those who abused God's people that He would judge their ways. Recalling the struggle in the womb of Esau and Jacob, the drama played out during the prophet's day. God knew who genuinely wished to walk in His ways, and He would not forget them.

**Jonah:** The Book of Jonah demonstrates God's sovereign ability to call a man to service, even when he would flee. His assignment was to lead a sinful city to repentance. Despite Jonah's disobedience, God was still able to orchestrate events and remove all obstacles to see evil eliminated and draw sinners back to Himself.

**Micah:** Micah came from humble surroundings to the courts of the rich and influential to pronounce a strong rebuke on those who would take advantage of the poor and downtrodden. The Lord will have His retribution with those who refuse to do as He requires of them.

**Nahum:** Nahum reminded the oppressors, who had once repented, that they had again turned from the Lord who had forgiven them of their sins. He declared that none were above His accountability and that the Lord would remove any and all who opposed Him.

**Habakkuk:** Habakkuk alerted Judah that their repeated hardness of heart and unwillingness to repent would not go unpunished. The Lord told his prophet that the Babylonians would be His method of reprisal. Habakkuk was forlorn, but knew that faith in God would be rewarded.

**Zephaniah:** Zephaniah saw the punishment of the Lord for those inhabitants of Jerusalem who continued to worship foreign Gods. The day of the Lord is coming, and the change that God requires must be sincere. A faithful God will bless the faithful remnant.

**Haggai:** Haggai reminded Israel that the Lord must be first in every part of their lives. The Lord will shake all the nations, but obedience will come to the Desire of All Nations (God), as the Lord of Hosts will fill His temple with glory. This is the promised blessing of the Lord.

**Zechariah:** Zechariah exhorted Israel to finish the work on the temple. He reminded them that this would be the house that their Messiah would enter to display His glory. Before He returned, the Lord expected obedience to the task at hand. Visions of the coming Lord inspired God's people.

**Malachi:** Malachi warned Israel that their privilege of knowing God was not an entitlement to continue corrupt practices. Israel's ongoing sin left that nation waiting for 400 years before the coming of the Messiah. Malachi confirmed that the day of the Lord's appearance, though long in coming, would happen suddenly.

## Appendix B

# New Testament Summary

**Matthew:** Matthew begins with the ancestry of Jesus to show His historical veracity, and then presents a highly detailed account of His unmistakable divinity. Matthew prioritizes our need to follow the Lord's commissioning as the model of life lived to its fullest.

**Mark:** Mark closely follows Jesus' life and ministry. The book starts by confirming Isaiah's prophecies about the Messiah from 700 years before the birth of Jesus. This is an action-filled account on the miracles, works, teachings, life, and person of Jesus.

**Luke:** Luke, as a doctor, gives a thorough reckoning of the life, works, and death of Jesus. Starting with a detailed analysis of the Messiah's heritage, Luke carefully relates key events with chronological accuracy. Emphasizing the Lord's equally divine and human nature, Luke confirms that Jesus is the only way to Heaven.

**John:** John declares that Jesus is God. He is the Word of God made into flesh. Everything that has ever been created was made through Him. In Him is light. John is the disciple closest to Jesus. He tells us of God's love for us and His means of salvation. John gives extensive coverage to the Passion Week and the details of Jesus' post-resurrection appearances.

**Acts:** Acts charts the course of the early Church. We see the apostles step out in faith, experience Pentecost, and the rapid expansion of Jews coming to faith. Paul is converted. Dynamic leaders join Paul and Peter as the Gospel spreads to the Gentiles and into the world.

**Romans:** Addressed to the church in Rome, Paul explores fundamental doctrines confirming God wants to bless us despite our sinfulness: God desires to forgive, not punish; God is a righteous God; grafting together of Jews and Gentiles into the olive tree of Israel.

**First Corinthians:** Corinth was the center of commerce for the Grecian peninsula at the time of Paul. It suffered terribly from misguided religious and cultural practices. Paul guides the church toward living a righteous life while existing in a pagan society. His words expound spiritual gifts, the resurrection, and a definitive treatise on love.

**Second Corinthians:** Following Paul's first letter, opposing forces have discredited the apostle. He sends Timothy to defend the faith, who turns the tide in the Lord's favor. Paul writes to thank, encourage, and strengthen their faith, calling them to reconcile with God and be watchful for false apostles.

**Galatians:** Galatia was the region between the Mediterranean and Black Seas. Paul confronts a church that has been schooled in the Gospel, but returns to a works mentality. The apostle shows no tolerance for such thinking and strongly defends his teachings. He directs such foolish constituents to remember that we are only justified by faith in God.

**Ephesians:** Ephesus sits on the western coast of present-day Turkey. Ephesians is a wake-up call to grab hold of the richness of life in Christ, finding our true identity as one new man in Him. Paul's words of lofty proportions exalt the Lord and inspire the body of believers to walk worthy of our call—to serve the Lord.

**Philippians:** Philippi sits above the northern coast of the Aegean Sea. Paul's letter of appreciation gives significant instructions on the unity of believers. Only in the excellent knowledge of Christ can we adequately express who He is to the world.

**Colossians:** Colossae is located in southwestern Asia Minor, or Turkey. Focusing on the headship and preeminence of Christ, through whom all things have been created, Paul tears down philosophical arguments. We are to set our hearts on things above and live peaceful, holy lives.

**First Thessalonians:** Thessalonica is found on the coast of the Aegean Sea in northern Greece. Upon receiving Timothy's report, Paul's sends a complimentary note of support against persecution. He maintains we need a strong work ethic as we live to please God. Paul briefly describes the coming of the Lord.

**Second Thessalonians:** Recognizing false doctrine being spread in the church, Paul weeds out the bad and gives appropriate teaching. He depicts Jesus and angelic hosts routing out evil; further personified as the lawless one who challenges God's authority with deception. We must hold to our tradition of faith and stand fast against unrighteousness.

**First Timothy:** Timothy has taken leadership of the church in Ephesus. Paul urges him to love from a pure heart and fight the good fight of faith in a glorious Gospel. Find qualified leaders, don't get sidetracked by those who depart, flee unrighteousness, and pursue righteousness.

**Second Timothy:** Writing Timothy from prison, Paul exhorts him to be faithful and unashamed of the Lord. He must be ready at all times to preach, testify, and endure hardships, a workman approved by God. He warns of perilous times ahead, describing a deceitful, vicious humanity.

**Titus:** Stationed on Crete, an island south of Greece, Paul charges Titus to set the new church in order; start by selecting mature elders. Titus is advised to teach sound doctrine based on obedience, accountability, and humility. Train the next generation to serve God.

**Philemon:** Paul's request of a prominent slave owner is a plea for forgiveness of a runaway slave. This one-time thief and deserter has come to faith. Appealing for mercy for "his son," Paul offers to pay the debt to assist in the redemption of one who was in sin, but now has found God.

**Hebrews:** Known as the faith chapter, Hebrews positions Jesus as Lord over the New Covenant. The fulfillment of Jesus as Messiah, our High Priest, even takes precedence over the covenant made with Moses. Jesus, though like us, is superior to the angels. He is the King of righteousness.

**James:** James is a man of action. He insists faith without works is dead. The deeds of a wise person are obvious, but we must watch what we say. We need to submit to God and curb our passions or they will lead to violence. To persevere requires patience, even in suffering.

**First Peter:** Peter was a fisherman. Jesus' resurrection gives us living hope. Since He is holy, so are we. He is the precious Cornerstone for the church. Submit to loved ones and authorities. Be willing to suffer for His goodness. Don't complain in trials. Know God's blessings. Live your life for God.

**Second Peter:** God's divine power provides all we need to escape corruption. As eyewitnesses to God's Majestic Glory, with an indisputable authority in the Holy Scriptures, stand certain of our heavenly calling and election. Be alert for false prophets and scoffers. Be ready for the day of the Lord.

**First John:** God is light, love, and life. As children of God we exemplify love as an imperative. The Lord, the Word, and the Holy Spirit are all we require. God's commands are not burdensome, for everyone born of God overcomes the world.

**Second John:** Knowing the truth, we are responsible to walk in truth. We are commanded to love one another. And this is love—that we walk in obedience to His commands.

**Third John:** Instructs us to stay in fellowship with believers.

**Jude:** To be a disciple is to build yourself up on your most holy faith. Pray in the power of the Holy Spirit to be strong so you can contend against the forces that attack the Body. Maintain a posture of readiness. Give glory to God. Jesus will present you as faultless before His Throne.

**Revelation:** Revelation tells the story, as given to John on the island of Patmos, of the consummation of the Kingdom of God. We see the Church through our Lord's eyes. We witness harsh tests, bitter trials. We gain insight about spiritual battles in the heavenlies. And finally, we see the triumph of Lord Jesus, who returns to lead us all to glory. Hallelujah!

## Majestic Glory Ministries

**M**ajestic Glory Ministries is dedicated to advancing the Kingdom of God by drawing individuals closer to the Lord, as we discover our divinely-ordained identity in Him. By promoting our identity as One New Man, Majestic Glory Ministries brings leaders and believers together to effectively address the most challenging and significant issues facing our communities in local, regional, national, and international settings.

Please visit us at: Awakening1.com.

# Notes

_____

_____

_____

_____

_____

_____

_____

_____

_____

_____

_____

_____

_____

# Notes

# Notes

# Notes

# Notes

# Notes

# Notes

# Notes

# Notes

# IN THE RIGHT HANDS, THIS BOOK WILL CHANGE LIVES!

Most of the people who need this message will not be looking for this book. To change their lives, you need to put a copy of this book in their hands.

> *But others (seeds) fell into good ground, and brought forth fruit, some a hundred-fold, some sixty-fold, some thirty-fold* (Matthew 13:8).

Our ministry is constantly seeking methods to find the good ground, the people who need this anointed message to change their lives. Will you help us reach these people?

> *Remember this—a farmer who plants only a few seeds will get a small crop. But the one who plants generously will get a generous crop* (2 Corinthians 9:6).

### EXTEND THIS MINISTRY BY SOWING
3 BOOKS, 5 BOOKS, 10 BOOKS, **OR MORE TODAY,**
AND BECOME A LIFE CHANGER!

Thank you,

Don Nori Sr., Founder
Destiny Image
Since 1982